A Closer Look at DOGS

A CLOSER LOOK BOOK

Published in the United States by
Gloucester Press in 1979

Designed by David Cook and
Associates and produced by
The Archon Press Limited
70 Old Compton Street
London W1V 5PA

First published in
Great Britain 1975 by
Hamish Hamilton
Children's Books Ltd
Garden House
57-59 Long Acre
London WC2E 9JL

The author wishes to
acknowledge the assistance
received from Juliet
Clutton-Brock, B.Sc., Ph.D.,
of the Dept. of Zoology,
British Museum (Natural History),
London, during the preparation
of this book.

Library of Congress
Catalog Card Number: 75–4390
ISBN (library edition): 0–531–01100–3
ISBN (paperback edition): 0–531–03447–X

Printed in Italy by Elcograf

A closer LOOK at DOGS

David Cook and Valerie Pitt

Illustrated by
Richard Orr and Shireen Faircloth

Gloucester Press | New York | 1979

What are dogs?

Can you imagine a chicken allowing itself to be taken for a walk on a lead? Or a cow curling up next to you by the fire? Or a cat guarding a factory? Or a pig herding sheep into a pen? Of all the animals man has domesticated, only dogs are intelligent enough, and friendly enough, to be trained to live and work closely with people.

Dogs are the best-known animals of all, kept by millions of people around the world. Yet they are also the most misunderstood animals. Because dogs are friendly and easily trained, many people forget they are animals. Dogs are often treated as though they were rather delicate human beings, or babies; little creatures to be fussed over, fed with choice scraps from the table and taken for dignified walks.

Stroll down any street and you will see this is true. Watch a dog out for a walk with its owner. Suddenly it spots another dog. Barking and wagging its tail, it darts forward in a rush of excitement. Soon it begins to sniff the other dog's hind quarters; a greeting that gives each dog important information about the other. But the owners become embarrassed (people don't behave like that!) and both move on, dragging their unhappy dogs with them.

If you want to find out what sort of animals dogs really are, what makes them superior members of the animal kingdom, you must first look at dogs in the wild – and particularly at wolves. For astonishing though it seems, all the Labradors and terriers, all the Pekes and pugs and poodles, and all the other breeds of domestic dogs were descended originally from wolf ancestors.

Discover how wolves behave in their natural environments – towering forests, mountain slopes, icy tundras – and you will discover that domestic dogs still behave in much the same way as their wild ancestors.

You will find the real answers to such questions as . . . Why do dogs sniff so much? Why do they roll over on their backs? Why do they always seem to urinate on lamp-posts or hedges and fences? Why do they make such loyal and loving pets to understanding owners?

First, let's look at the dog's place in the animal world. Along with hyenas, cats, and four other groups, dogs belong to the order of animals known as the Carnivora. Carnivores are hunters, they survive mainly by killing other animals for food. As flesh-eaters, the carnivores generally have lithe bodies for catching their prey; and powerful jaws, strong claws and sharp teeth for tearing and eating it.

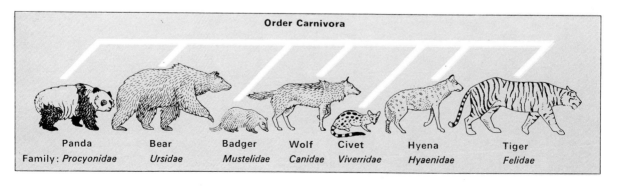

Order Carnivora

| Panda | Bear | Badger | Wolf | Civet | Hyena | Tiger |
| Family: *Procyonidae* | *Ursidae* | *Mustelidae* | *Canidae* | *Viverridae* | *Hyaenidae* | *Felidae* |

The 'typical' dogs

Cats, hyenas, dogs: quite different sorts of animals survive mainly by hunting other creatures for food. To make it easier to distinguish between them the order Carnivora is divided into families.

Dogs belong to the family called the Canidae. We see some members of this family all the time: the domestic breeds, such as poodles and German shepherds. These are dogs which have been bred by man.

But the family Canidae also contains some dogs we rarely see – the wild dogs: wolves, jackals, foxes, raccoon dogs, bush dogs, coyotes and many others.

Some members of this large dog family are more closely-related than others. Scientists can tell this by examining their skulls, teeth and jaws. Domestic dogs, for instance, are much more like wolves than they are like foxes. So the dog family is separated into closely-related groups.

The group Canis contains the 'typical' dogs. They are the wolves, the jackals, the coyotes, and the domestic dogs. You can see some of the similarities of these 'typical' dogs just by looking at them. They are all medium-size animals with lean legs. They all have long muzzles and tapered jaws. They all have erect ears. And they all have 'pelts,' coats of fur or short coarse hair, with the same basic coloration.

Yet when you compare these dogs with some breeds of domestic dogs, there are surprising differences too; think of the floppy-eared spaniel, or the short-legged waddling dachshund, or the spotted Dalmatian. Think of the Mexican hairless dog: it has no hair at all. Are these dogs really related to the powerful magnificent wolves? In fact, all these differences are the results of human needs and whims, and are the results of selective breeding for characteristics such as floppy ears and short legs that are favored by dog owners.

Despite these outward differences, domestic dogs still behave much like wolves. Hard to believe? Let's look and see.

Wolf
Wolves are the largest, most spectacular wild dogs. They are found in North America, Europe and Asia. They hunt large animals and, like all dogs, will also feed on carrion – the rotting remains of dead animals.

Coyote
Coyotes look like small wolves. They live on the North American plains where their startling sing-song howls may be heard for miles. Coyotes will eat almost anything.

Jackal
Jackals are found in Africa and Asia. Smaller and shyer than wolves, they hunt small animals and also eat carrion.

Domestic dog
Domestic dogs live wherever man makes his home. Dingos are a variety of domestic dog, found in Australia, which have returned to living in the wild.

The all-rounder

All wild animals fight an unending battle for survival, every hour and every day of their lives. Death may come suddenly, in the form of a surprise attack by a more powerful animal or it may come more slowly, from lack of food, harsh weather, injuries, or other hazards.

In this constant fight for survival, the most successful animals are those which can adapt to changing conditions; those which do not have to rely on a single source of food, or a particular environment. Dogs are among the most adaptable animals of all. They are all-rounders:

- able to exist on fruit, insects, lizards, fish, carrion, and even garbage when meat is not available, and able to go for many days without eating at all
- able to withstand burning heat or bitter cold
- able to live in quite different types of terrain: the forbidding tundras, forests, mountainous areas, open plains.

Then, too, dogs have a supreme advantage. They number among the hunters of the world, not the hunted. This gives them great physical benefits: strong agile bodies, long fine-boned legs for running, padded toes for treading perilous rocks and slippery ice, slashing jaws, strong claws and teeth. And to top it all, 'hidden weapons' for hunting out their prey – acute senses of smell and hearing.

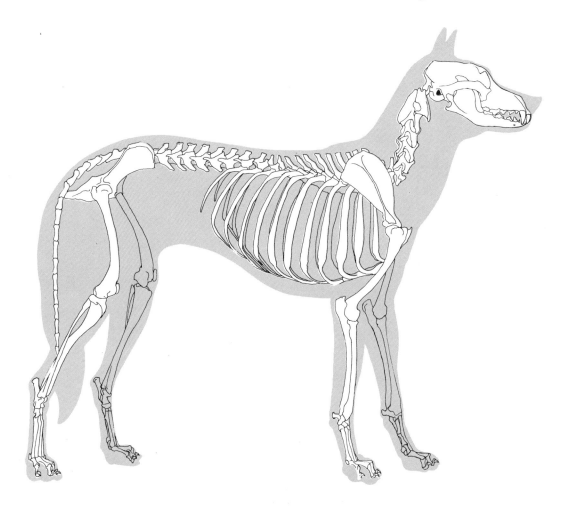

Effective jaws

Cats usually hunt alone so they need a powerful bite in order to grip and kill prey quickly. Wolves hunt in packs. They slash and tear at their prey until they kill it. Compare the wolf's skull with the cat's, on the right. The dog's jaws are long and tapered and perfectly adapted for ripping at prey.

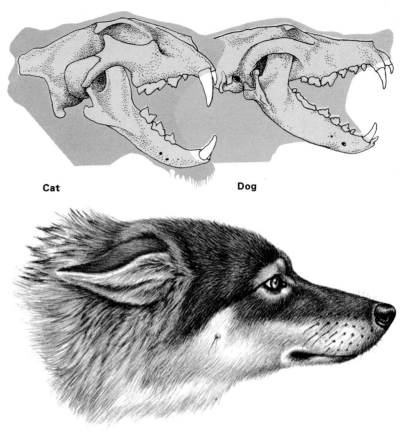

Cat   Dog

Remarkable senses

Dogs hunt prey over long distances. In order to find their food dogs must track down animals by scent and hearing. Dogs have astonishingly keen senses. They may be able to pick up the scent of prey over a mile away; smell one drop of blood in a bucketful of water; and hear very high-pitched sounds. The dog has large ears; and a long muzzle, which runs from its eyes to its nostrils, to house the many important scent nerves. Cats hunt mainly by sight. Their skulls are shorter and more rounded to allow for larger eyes.

Teeth for tearing

Wolves and other wild dogs have specialized teeth for dealing with their prey. They have four long fangs, or canine teeth (one in each corner of the jaw) which interlock with the incisors next to them. Deadly in the hunt, these teeth are used for gripping, tearing and slashing at prey. The carnassial teeth, next to them, move from side to side like the blades of shears, so the wolf can chew and cut through bones. The large rather flattened molars then crush and grind up the bones and meat.

In the case of many domestic dogs selective breeding for looks has resulted in much less effective jaws and teeth than the wolf's.

The German shepherd is one of the most wolf-like domestic dogs but its jaws are now shorter and its teeth smaller and crowded together.

The jaws of the Pekinese have become so squashed there may be no room for some of the teeth.

Some bulldogs cannot hunt at all because their bite has become so distorted.

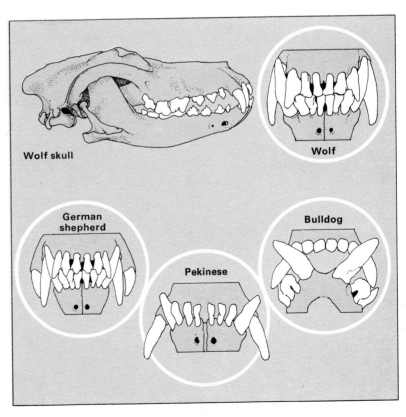

Wolf skull

Wolf

German shepherd

Pekinese

Bulldog

Living in packs

Of all the dogs, wolves are the most powerful hunters. Just the sight of one – fur bristling, ears pricked, eyes gleaming – is enough to send hares and mice shivering to safety.

But when wolves are hungry they are on the alert for much bigger prey: caribou, moose (or elk), deer, mountain sheep, buffalo. Because they hunt animals which are usually much larger than themselves, wolves rarely hunt alone. As in all battles, survival and safety lie in numbers. For this reason wolves live and hunt in packs.

Most wolf packs have six to eight members. The pack is usually made up of a family group: male and female parents, full-grown offspring and, often, young pups too. Each pack lives and hunts in its own territory, or range, which is only invaded by other wolves at their peril. On the Arctic tundra, or on rolling steppes and prairies, the range may cover hundreds of miles. In wooded or mountainous areas there may be much less territory to go round.

A wolf pack is a formidable hunting group, but it does not have everything its own way: prey animals also have defensive weapons at their disposal – speed of foot, kicking hooves, dangerous horns. So hunting is not always an easy matter, not just a question of racing up to an animal and over-powering it. It is much more a battle of wits and endurance. This makes it vital for members of a pack to live and hunt together smoothly, as a team. The way they manage to do this is one of the most astounding things about dog society.

The pack
A wolf pack is usually made up of a family group: male and female parents and full-grown offspring. The parents generally mate each year and raise young pups who in time also become full members of the pack.

Whether they are wolves or human beings, members of any group must first of all be capable of showing friendship and respect for each other, otherwise fighting may cause the group to split up. Wolves grow up in a way which ensures that a bond of attachment is formed between members of a pack. This bond keeps the pack together.

But a bond, by itself, is not enough to keep order within a group. There also has to be a leader and a chain of command so that each member knows what its role is and what jobs it should be doing. In a wolf pack the chain of command is very strict: it has to be, for if there were no strong dogs capable of controlling and organizing the others the group would hunt haphazardly and might easily starve.

The most important member of the pack is the leader, the top dog. It heads the hunting team, eats first, and dominates every other member of the pack. It shows its strength and superiority all the time in many different ways and its position is recognized and respected by all the members of the team. Next in line is the second-in-command. It is dominated only by the leader. In turn, it dominates all the members in the ranks below. This pattern is followed all through the pack. Because each member knows its place, the whole pack can work together smoothly. Stray domestic dogs, which roam together in packs, have a similar chain of command.

How do wolves find and learn their place in the pack? The process begins soon after they are born.

The chain of command
Pack members are usually different sizes and have different temperaments. There is nearly always a cringing creature, picked on by the others. If the pack is set upon by other wolves, this straggler is the first to be attacked; this gives the stronger wolves time to escape. Differences between pack members make it possible for them to work as a team, and to have an orderly chain of command. Here, the no. 1 wolf, the pack leader, is the male parent. The no. 2 wolf is the top female, the mother. The no. 3 wolf is a male. The no. 4 wolf is a female. The no. 5 wolf is a male of weak temperament. If the leader is injured or grows too old to keep command it may be torn to pieces by the others. Only an efficient team can hunt successfully, and the chain of command may shift round completely. Wolves are always on the alert for weaknesses in the others, trying to steal food or dominate each other with threatening gestures. In this way the young rise up in the pack.

The first days

Each year, around February, she-wolves (females) over the age of twenty-two months become fertile. If a she-wolf mates with a male wolf at this time she usually becomes pregnant and just over two months later will bear her pups.

For a mated pair, the weeks before the birth of their pups are a restless, busy time. They must find a safe den to rear their young. The den must be near water, for neither the mother nor her pups will be able to travel far to drink and it must be snug and sheltered. Often wolves choose a hollow amongst trees or rocks for their den. In the deepest part of the den they scrape out a nest. If they have to leave the pups alone, the young will not be strong enough to climb out of this nest and wander into danger.

Domestic bitches (female dogs) often scrape out nests when they are pregnant. They have inherited this trait from their wolf ancestors.

The rest of the pack, made up of full-grown offspring from the previous year, accompany their parents to the den. When they are twenty-two months old, they may mate and form new packs. Now they will help their parents to provide food for the new litter.

Eventually the she-wolf, who has been pampered and well-fed by her mate, settles herself into the den to give birth to the pups.

The newly-born pup

A pup is born inside a protective fluid-filled sac which the mother bites open to free it. Then she eats the sac to help restore the body fluids she has lost during the birth. The puppy is connected to the mother by a cord which she soon severs.

Feeding time

The she-wolf may have four or five pups though not all may survive. New-born pups are bedraggled creatures which can neither see nor hear. The mother licks them dry then they huddle close to her warm body and start to suck her milk. Even at this stage the most superior pups can be spotted. They are the first to find their mother's nipples and feed.

Smelling

Smell, the most important sense, is the first to develop. After sucking only once a pup can recognize its mother's nipples. After two weeks it learns to recognize its litter-mates by smell.

Seeing

A pup's eyes open around the end of its second week but it cannot see clearly yet. Its eyes are placed on the sides of its head for all-round vision. This is important for following the movements of prey during a hunt.

Hearing

A pup begins to hear when it is about three weeks old. It is frightened by a loud noise and quickly crawls away from it. Later, its acute hearing will help the wolf to detect the movements of prey. Domestic dogs can pick up sounds long before their owners and hear shrill sounds that humans cannot hear at all.

Bring a dog a bone

Often the father wolf brings the she-wolf food while she is suckling the pups. At three weeks old the pups may start to play outside the den. The father brings them bones to gnaw and sharpen their teeth on. Domestic pups lack the fatherly care that wolf pups get, for usually male and female domestic dogs are only brought together to mate. The bitch then rears the pups alone.

11

Forming vital bonds

Three weeks after their birth, wolf pups venture into the strange exciting world outside the den. They breathe crisp air and feel the warmth of the sun, they watch curiously as small creatures scurry across the landscape, they snuffle and sniff everything around them, including their brothers and sisters and the adults of the pack, learning to distinguish their different smells.

Now there are many lessons to be learned. In a few weeks time the pups will leave the den area with the rest of the pack. Before then, vital bonds of attachment and respect for other members of the pack must be formed.

Wolf pups form their first bonds with the adults, with their mother who suckles them and with their father and full-grown brothers and sisters who help lick them clean and look after them. Like human babies, the pups respond to this affection. But they must also quickly learn to show respect for the adults' superiority and strength. If they do not they will be hounded unmercifully.

By the fourth week the pups are receiving semi-digested food as well as milk. The adults may trot tirelessly for 15 miles or more to hunt and bring back fresh pieces of meat for the young. The adults swallow the meat and half-digest it in their stomachs, then they vomit it up and pass it to the pups from their mouths. As soon as the adults return to the den the pups rush up to them and nuzzle them around the mouth to obtain the food. This feeding ritual helps to strengthen the developing social bonds.

Later, this same nose-nudging gesture will become a sign of respect and submission between pack members and their superiors. In domestic dogs nose-nudging is a similar sign of respect to their superiors, their owners. It means they want an affectionate stroke.

Social bonds also begin to form among the litter-mates. For three weeks they have crawled and cuddled close together in the den. Now,

Showing respect
The pups must learn to respect their father's authority, and also to recognize their place as very junior members of the pack.

as their curiosity stirs, they begin to explore and play together and they begin to copy their parents' behavior; they learn to howl, to pounce, to snap at and chase small animals.

The pups also start to fight among themselves. Scrambling, sniffing, pushing, biting, each one tries to dominate the others. In the process they begin to learn the strengths and weaknesses of their brothers and sisters, a first step towards deciding superiority.

If one pup seems much stronger during a fight, the weaker pup will turn over on its back to signal its helplessness. With this gesture it shows its most vulnerable area, its throat and belly. This action is usually enough to settle a dispute for it blocks the more aggressive dog's instinct to bite.

Adults also turn over on their backs as a sign of submission to superior members of the pack. This behavior helps to prevent outright fighting and to preserve harmony in the chain of command. Domestic dogs also use this gesture when they feel threatened by stronger dogs or by their owners or simply when they want affection.

By the time they are three months old, wolf pups have formed lasting bonds. From now on they will only show friendship to members of their own pack; they will be a united team.

The only exception to this will be when two strange wolves court in the fertile season. During mating itself, the pair become physically joined together and this 'tie' may last half an hour or longer. Neither male nor female can break it. This may be nature's way of ensuring that a bond is formed between strange wolves which would normally be aggressive to each other. Once a bond had been formed in this way, the pair can form their own pack.

For domestic dogs, the first three months is also the most crucial time for forming bonds with human beings. Without plenty of friendly contacts with people during this time, they will always be shy.

Learning their place

When the pups are about three months old, and the bonds between them have become firm, they leave the den area for good.

For the rest of the summer they will travel with the pack. Although they now eat meat, the pups are not yet strong enough to hunt. They rest at camps along the route while the adults hunt food for them.

Now the serious business of learning begins. The father wolf, the pack leader, usually plays the important role of teacher. He chases the pups and encourages them to chase him, he hides and forces them to seek him out, he circles and pounces, he appears suddenly – out of nowhere – in a surprise ambush. In this way he teaches the pups basic tactics for the hunt.

Games and fights between the pups themselves also become serious, for the matter of superiority must be settled so that each pup knows its place in the chain of command and can show the appropriate behavior to its seniors. There will be no time to sort out differences later on when the pups begin to hunt with their parents, for the survival of the pack will depend on its ability to hunt efficiently. If it cannot hunt as a team, the pack will starve.

This training period is also very important in the life of the domestic dog. It is at this age that it needs and respects discipline.

Tests of strength
The weaknesses and strengths of their litter-mates are tested time and time again by the pups during their training period. Some may become bitten and bloody from the battles, but it is in this way that the pups learn their place in the chain of command.

Learning tactics
When they are a few months older the pups will become part of the hunting team. They will have to scent out herd animals over long distances, follow their movements carefully and give chase. In order to hunt successfully they may have to circle their prey or pounce in a surprise ambush. Pups learn these tricks by playing hunting games and by following their father's example.

Demonstrating their place

Once their place in the pack order has been settled, wolves have special ways of demonstrating their superiority or inferiority to other members. This helps to prevent unnecessary fighting and conserve energy for the important business of hunting. Wolves use tail movements and body postures as 'signals' to show confidence or fear when they are threatened. These movements are associated with their most important sense, smell. Each wolf has its own particular smell which is recognized by all the others. Some of the most powerful scent-producing glands are situated around the anus.

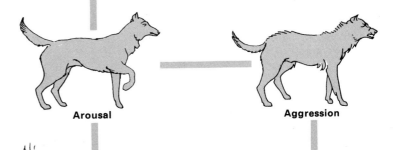

Aggression

Superior animals lift their tails to show their dominance (a warning that they are not to be trifled with), raise their hackles, and bare their jaws to show threatening teeth.

Arousal

Aggression

Play-begging

Aggression/fear

Play-begging

Fear

Choice of action

In the large picture above you can see the posture a wolf may adopt when it has been threatened by another member of the pack. For a second it is undecided about how to react and its body shows its indecision: its tail is clamped between its legs, which shows fear; but its jaws are opened in a gape, which is a sign of aggression and defence. Depending on its place in the chain of command the wolf will finally react in one of two ways. If it is a superior member of the pack it will show aggression; if it is an inferior member it will show submission.

Play-submission

Fear/submission

Submission

Animals lower down in the chain of command show fear when they are threatened. They hunch up their bodies trying to make themselves look as small as possible and thrust their tails between their legs to signify their submission. If the stronger dog seems about to bite, they roll over on their backs. This reaction is usually enough to avert an outright fight.

Submission

Communicating

Prides of lions, colonies of ants, human families, wolf packs . . . all the creatures which live together in groups must be able to communicate among themselves.

Members of a wolf pack live, rest, hunt, feed and spend most of their time together so pups must learn to recognize moods and messages passed on from the upper ranks. If the chain of command is to work smoothly, these messages must be understood quickly.

One of the most important ways in which wolves communicate is through their individual scents. A pack leader can quickly dominate the group by lifting its tail. Scent makes it easy for wolves to follow and keep up with each other too, for they sweat through their paws and leave scent trails behind them.

But wolves, and domestic dogs, also communicate in other ways; they use facial expressions and their voices to pass on messages. And they indulge in small 'ceremonies' just as we do. When wolves meet they nudge each other's mouths with their muzzles. Nose-nudging may follow a short absence, or even a nap, but this ritual keeps up the bond of attachment and helps show respect for more senior members. Before they set off on a hunt, wolves often huddle close together and nuzzle their leader.

Facial expressions
A pack leader often keeps other members in line merely by looking at them in certain ways. Here, the leader's expression changes from (1) a steady tolerant stare; (2) to anxiety; (3) to suspicion; (4) to real threat.

1.

2.

3.

4.

The howl
This famous wolf cry is used as a friendly greeting between members of a pack. Howling is also used as a warning to other packs. The message is clear. 'Stay away!'

Marking territory

Wolves howl more often than they bark because the sound carries further over their large territories. They have other ways to warn off stray wolves too; the leader and other superior members mark the territory by urinating on rocks, trees and other boundaries. Their scent is a sign of 'ownership.'

Leg-lifting

Domestic dogs bark and snarl when strangers enter their territory – their homes and gardens. This territorial instinct makes many pets perfect 'alarm systems.' Domestic dogs also act like members of a pack, lifting their legs and marking boundaries around their homes. The next dog that smells this ownership claim on a post or fence covers it with a spray of its own.

Part of the team

By the time winter comes the pups have grown almost as large as their parents. Although they will not be full-grown wolves until the end of their first year, they can trot for many miles with the others. Now, at last, they have become full members of the pack, able to show the sort of behavior which befits an efficient hunting team.

Wolves may track their prey by following hoof trails and droppings. They may come across an animal or a herd of deer or caribou by chance. More often they scent out their prey. As soon as the pack picks up the scent of prey it stops; ears, eyes, and noses are all pointed in the direction of the scent. Then, with a sudden dart, the pack turns and heads towards it. As they come closer to the prey the wolves may fan out. Stealthily now they begin to stalk, trying to get as close as possible before they are spotted.

Now the hunters and the hunted face each other. This is the most critical stage of the hunt. Large powerful prey such as moose may stand their ground and the wolves may decide to use ambush tactics or give up altogether. Herd prey, such as deer or caribou, may stampede in panic. Picking out a stumbling animal, or one which is lagging behind, the pack leaps forward and the chase is on.

If they catch up within the first few minutes of the chase the wolves attack, ripping and tearing at the prey's most vulnerable areas, its flanks, belly, nose and neck. Then the feast begins.

Wolf against Moose

No predator, whatever its size, will risk injury to itself, and the sharp hooves of the moose are daunting even to wolves.

A survey in Canada has shown that of 130 encounters between wolves and moose, only six prey were killed. Some moose stood their ground, even when the wolves tried ambush techniques. In the end, the wolves retreated in search of easier prey.

Helpful hunters

Wolves are efficient killers but not stupid ones. They aim for the animals they stand most chance of catching. This usually means the weakest members of a herd; the old, the injured, or the very young, for strong prey animals can often out-run their hunters. Because a wolf pack usually chooses weak prey it actually helps a herd to preserve its strongest, healthiest members to continue the breed.

The domestication of wolves

Wolves were the first animals to be domesticated by man. When you consider the fierce way they fight for existence in the wild, it seems almost impossible that wolves could ever have been tamed by human beings. But, in fact, this may not have been a particularly difficult task for early peoples because they lived very similar lives themselves; for them hunting was also the main way of surviving.

Tribes roamed the wild countryside, making temporary camps and killing whatever animals they could find with primitive weapons. Sometimes they caused stampedes among grazing herds so the animals would panic and some could be driven into traps or over cliffs.

By following trails, the wolf packs which competed with the tribes for food could sometimes provide themselves with a free meal, the carcasses of animals killed by humans which would pile up in ravines or around camp sites. In this way some of the wolf hunters and the human hunters could have become associated.

In the beginning, humans may have raised young wolf pups whose parents had been killed for food or fur. If their own kind are not around, wolf pups will attach themselves readily to humans during the early bonding stage, so it is not hard to imagine how a wolf pup could be raised by a human being. In the eyes of the orphaned pup, or the wolves which were later born in captivity, man naturally took the place of the pack leader; he became the ultimate authority to be obeyed and pleased in return for food and protection. The tamed wolf would help in the hunt and guard the camp, or territory, from enemies because this sort of behavior would also be quite natural to it.

Hunters and guards

It is believed that some wolves were tamed by man as early as 20,000 years ago. At this stage of domestication, wolves were used mainly as assistants in the hunt and as guards. Both these activities would be very natural for them. As pack animals, the wolves would instinctively work well in groups trying to please the human hunter, the 'pack leader.' Using their remarkable senses of smell and hearing they could lead humans to prey animals they would probably not be able to locate themselves. During the hunt they would encircle prey or drive them into traps. And during the kill they would use their natural weapons, snapping jaws and slashing teeth. Guarding the human camps would come just as naturally, for wolves would regard them as their own territory and defend them vigorously. With their acute hearing they would be able to detect strangers or dangerous animals long before the humans.

Scavengers

The early hunters and wandering tribes found wolves helpful in other ways too. At the temporary camps they made over their hunting range, the carcasses of the animals they had killed for food and fur would pile up in evil-smelling heaps. Wolves, and all the other members of the dog family, will feed on almost anything including the rotting remains of dead animals. These adaptable feeding habits are, of course, one of the prime reasons why they survive so successfully in different habitats. The tame wolves, and wild strays attracted by the stench surrounding the camps, would act as efficient garbage collectors, polishing off the carrion. In this way, the wolves also helped to keep their human companions healthy, for carrion attracts plagues of flies which can carry and spread such diseases as cholera and dysentery. Today, native tribes that live in primitive encampments, still find wild dogs valuable as scavengers. In Australia, the dingo often performs this task.

New roles

Gradually the way of life changed for early peoples. They learned to raise crops and grow food; they learned how to keep herds of goats, cattle and sheep to provide meat and milk. Now it was no longer necessary to continually wander in search of food in order to stay alive. This was a great step forward in civilization for it meant that people could live together in more permanent settlements and devote time to pursuits other than hunting. As man evolved from a nomad to a home-dweller, the role of the wolf changed too. By about 5,000 B.C. a tame stock of wolves had developed, and man had learned that by selective breeding he could encourage or discourage certain characteristics, such as fierceness or friendliness, in his dogs. In this way different types of dogs were bred for different purposes; still as hunters, but also as sheep herders, house-guards and pets. Dogs had become 'man's best friend.'

The surprising variety of dogs

Greyhounds, dachshunds, Pekinese, bulldogs, sheepdogs . . . there are hundreds of breeds of domestic dogs and they all look different. How could all these different dogs have descended from wolves ?

The answer lies in what is known as selective breeding. When early peoples realized what useful allies wolves made, how adept they were at hunting, herding and guarding and how strongly these instincts were passed on to their puppies, they began to experiment.

A shepherd, for instance, may have noticed that two dogs showed a keener sense of protection towards his sheep than the other more aggressive dogs did. By mating these two dogs together, or with a similarly protective dog in the neighborhood, he found he was able to encourage this quality further in the litter-mates. When he then mated these puppies with each other he found that their pups, in turn, had more pronounced instincts.

Cross-breeding of closely-related animals or litter-mates eventually resulted in different types of dogs. These dogs looked quite different from their original wolf ancestors because variations in build, jaw size, leg length, tail carriage, color and temperament had been passed on and intensified from generation to generation over thousands of years. Under natural conditions this would not have happened.

Natural selection

In nature only the fittest animals survive. The fittest animals are those which are best adapted to their environments. Such adaptations show themselves in variations of such characteristics as size, color, strength and temperament. In a wolf pack these variations make it possible for the chain of command to run smoothly. They also ensure that the wolves with the most successful variations will live and breed the next generation. Useful variations are handed down from parents to offspring. A light color in Arctic regions, for example, may mean an animal can hide and hunt more efficiently. Sometimes a 'mistake' occurs in the variations that are handed down. Pups may be born with abnormalities such as short legs or over-large heads. Usually these abnormalities are harmful and tend to weaken the animal. As a result it dies before it becomes fully grown and capable of mating. The abnormality is therefore not passed on. Under artificial conditions, such as selective breeding, abnormalities can turn out to be useful variations. They can be used to produce new types of dogs.

Timber wolf

Arctic wolf

Selective breeding

Once man began to experiment with the breeding of tamed wolves, variations became highly controlled rather than natural. Such variations as short legs or short jaws, which resulted from constant cross-breeding and inter-breeding, would not have been passed on in the wild because they would have been unsuitable tools for coping with the hazards of the environment. Wolves with such feeble and abnormal variations would have died off quickly in the fierce struggle for survival. Under the artificial conditions in which wolves lived with man, however, there was no struggle for survival. Food, shelter, and mates were automatically provided by the human pack leader. Animals with 'domestic' variations survived to breed and pass on their characteristics. Experts believe that all the different domestic dogs evolved from four basic wolf stocks that lived in different parts of the world. These wolves had different variations in size, color and looks adapted to the places where they lived. In the chart, on the right, you can see a family tree which shows the sort of dogs which descended from each stock. It is only a guide, of course, for there has been so much 'crossing of the lines' over the past 7,000 years or so that it is impossible to trace exact lines back. The North American wolf is believed to be the ancestor of the Eskimo dogs. Even today they still look much like wolves. The Chinese wolf is thought to be the ancestor of chows, toy spaniels and Pekinese. The Indian wolf was probably the ancestor of a large group that includes greyhounds and Salukis. The European wolf was probably the ancestor of sheepdogs and terriers. Selective breeding of dogs can be helpful to man; it has produced all these different dogs which can tackle jobs people find hard to do alone. But selective breeding can sometimes be harmful to the dogs themselves. It can produce defects such as breathing troubles, weak jaws and eye defects, and nervous natures.

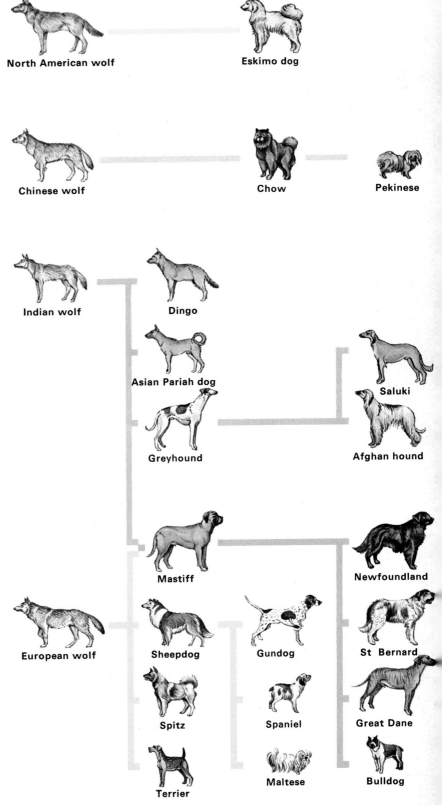

North American wolf — Eskimo dog

Chinese wolf — Chow — Pekinese

Indian wolf — Dingo — Asian Pariah dog — Greyhound — Saluki — Afghan hound

European wolf — Mastiff — Newfoundland — Sheepdog — Gundog — St Bernard — Spitz — Spaniel — Great Dane — Terrier — Maltese — Bulldog

Changing needs

Early on in his breeding experiments man decided that he wanted his dogs to have certain well-defined qualities so they could help him with particular jobs. Fierceness was encouraged in some dogs so they would make good guards and defend property; endurance was encouraged in others so they could pull heavy loads; the herding instinct was encouraged in others so they could round up sheep.

Later, selective breeding enabled people to develop dogs with special variations for more specific purposes. Hunters in the vast desert areas of Egypt and Arabia needed speedy animals that could pursue their prey by sight. They developed lean swift greyhounds for this job.

When it was no longer so necessary to breed animals to hunt food, some dogs were bred for less vital purposes. Pekinese, pomeranians and other toy dogs were bred for certain looks that appealed to their owners. As well-cared-for pets they were able to survive.

Some dogs were also bred for sporting purposes. Sportsmen liked the thrill of the chase, even though they did not necessarily eat the animals their dogs caught. To breed a dog that could draw badgers out from their underground homes, breeders had to develop a mixture of variations. They had to produce a dog that combined braveness of spirit, with short legs (for penetrating a badger's nest) and a long muzzle (for scenting out its prey and biting it quickly if necessary). At the end of many generations of selective breeding, the courageous short-legged, long-faced dachshund was produced. Its German name means badger dog.

Hawk and hound
In medieval and later times hunters carried hawks perched on their wrists. These were used to attack game birds such as pheasants and partridges. The game was first flushed out of marshy thickets by spaniels that had well-adapted waterproof coats for hunting in such areas.

A new weapon

With the invention of guns, a different type of sporting dog was needed. Early guns had to be reloaded after every shot. The noise of the first shot would frighten game birds and they would quickly fly off, so the hunter had to make sure that his first shot hit home. In order to do this, he needed a dog with good senses of hearing and smell which could scent out game, track it quietly, then 'point' out its position to the hunter. Pointers were developed for this purpose. Moving slowly and silently, they would freeze when they approached game and point their muzzles, bodies and tails in its direction.

Retrieving game

By the 19th century, shot-guns had become greatly improved weapons. Several shots could now be fired in succession. As guns changed, so did the requirements of the sportsmen. Now they needed dogs capable of finding game birds that fell into lakes or other hard-to-reach places, and of carrying them back. Retrievers were bred for this purpose. They had good sight for spotting where the birds fell, they could swim well, and they had specially 'soft' mouths for carrying the game without damaging it.

All-purpose dogs

Today's sportsmen have reaped the benefits of generations of selective breeding. They can keep and train dogs that are adapted for many sporting purposes. One of the most popular all-purpose breeds is the Labrador. Labradors can flush out game birds; they can spot where they fall once they have been shot; and they can retrieve them in their mouths. Labradors have special coats that are adapted to resist water and bad weather. This means they can successfully retrieve birds from lakes and ponds and hunt in marshy areas. Because they are also very intelligent animals, Labradors are often trained as police dogs and guide-dogs.

Working dogs

Guiding the blind . . . herding sheep . . . tracking criminals and missing persons . . . pulling heavy loads over barren ice . . . guarding homes and factories . . . scenting out people buried under snowdrifts, or wounded on the battlefield . . . hunting rats and other pests that destroy crops: dogs' sociable and adaptable natures have made it possible for them to be trained for many highly specialized jobs.

In our own time, dogs have been parachuted with regiments on to battlefields and have even been rocketed into space; two Russian dogs survived seventeen orbits of the earth in a space capsule.

Working dogs need special qualities. Female Labradors, boxers, and Shepherds generally make the best guide-dogs for the blind because they have calm gentle natures. Male dogs of these breeds are usually more aggressive. Guide-dogs are trained to ignore all distractions, from heavy traffic to the sound of alarm bells.

The scenting abilities of St. Bernard's, Shepherds and bloodhounds are highly developed. These breeds are trained to track missing persons. Before it starts to track, a dog is often given an object to sniff, such as a glove, to familiarize it with the person's scent. Such a dog is even capable of detecting the difference in scent between one human being's sweat and another's.

The trainer of any kind of working dog assumes the role of pack leader. With kind but firm leadership he shows that he is in command. Because it receives rewards, such as food, protection and affection, the dog instinctively obeys and tries to please the leader. It shows its respect by responding immediately to a single word or slight gesture.

Sheepdogs

German-type shepherd dogs, which could protect flocks of sheep, cattle, or reindeer, were probably among the first dogs to be bred by man. Later, sheepdogs such as collies were bred to control and round up flocks of sheep. Collies often act like wolf pack-leaders, using a steady intimidating 'stare' to get sheep moving in the direction they want them to go. Sheepdogs may work alone or in pairs. They are trained to round up sheep, drive them into pens, single out separate animals from the flock, and track down sheep which become lost or trapped in snow. Long-haired sheepdogs were originally bred in Russia. Their shaggy coats protected them from the bitter winds that swept across the steppes, and their 'fringes' protected their eyes from the glare of sunlight on snow. These dogs were developed to combine strength and intelligence. In this way they were able to protect and control sheep.

Police dogs

Shepherds, Labradors, boxers, and Great Danes are highly intelligent dogs and are the breeds most often chosen for training by the police. They are used to sniff out hidden drugs at airports and docks, to control crowds and to track down criminals, as well as many other tasks. Police dogs must learn behavior that many human beings would find extraordinarily difficult so they need very specialized and patient training. If they are to learn they must respect and trust their human pack-leaders without reservation. Well-trained dogs will literally jump through burning hoops for their handlers. They will remain calm under gun-fire and among large disorderly crowds of people. They will refuse food offered to them by strangers, for it may be poisoned. They will track down criminals but let go their hold the moment they are commanded to. And they will defend their handlers from attack under dangerous and highly-charged conditions.

Sledge dogs

Dogs have been used to pull heavy loads since the earliest times. The best known of today's sledge dogs are the huskies, which usually work together in teams. Of all the dogs, huskies are the ones which most resemble wild wolves. This is because they are often mated with wolves to intensify characteristics such as hardiness and endurance. These qualities are vital for coping with the harsh environments in which they live. Teams of huskies may have to pull extremely heavy loads over vast distances of barren ice in the frozen Arctic regions. Sometimes the dogs are hitched to the sledge in a fan position, with a rope attached to each dog. Sometimes they are harnessed in pairs with a leader in front to guide the team. It was thanks to the huskies' endurance that Europeans were able to explore the Arctic at the beginning of this century, for without huskies, no vehicle could cross such terrain.

A dog's life

Most of the millions of dogs that are kept by people all around the world are not used for hunting, sporting, or working purposes. They are kept as friendly companions and pets.

Some of these pets are happy, well-adjusted animals that are loyal and loving to their owners, some are miserable pathetic creatures that cringe in fear or snap with aggression, some are so spoiled they seem to rule their owners.

Why the differences? They are usually the results of different sorts of behavior on the part of the human owners.

Someone who understands the social nature of dogs, who understands that they are basically pack animals which respond to firm protective leadership by trying to please the leader, usually raises a friendly obedient dog which becomes a favorite member of the human family pack. Someone who does not understand this and who gives his dog a pat one moment and a harsh clout the next, will probably raise a fearful or withdrawn animal. Someone who continually spoils his dog and allows it to do as it likes, may raise an animal that becomes so aggressive it tries to dominate the family pack.

Tests show that raising dogs as 'naturally' as possible usually results in happy pets and happy owners.

The first weeks
Like the wolf pup in the wild, a domestic pup spends most of the time during its first three weeks sleeping and feeding. It needs the comfort of its mother. For the next five weeks it needs to play, fight, and get to know its litter-mates. This ensures that it will not be too fearful or too aggressive towards other dogs when it is older. If it is to develop normal friendly relationships with human beings too, it must also have plenty of affectionate contacts with people.

The bonding stage
A puppy should be bought when it is between eight and twelve weeks old. If it has had friendly contacts with people up to this point it will be lively and curious. If it hasn't, it will always be shy, withdrawn and difficult to train. The next few weeks are critical for it is now that the pup forms lasting bonds with its owner. Firm, kind, consistent treatment ensures a friendly bond. Each time it learns 'good' behavior it should be rewarded with love; when it does something wrong it should be firmly told 'No!' and given a shake.

Growing up

Because they do not usually have to 'struggle' to survive like wolves, domestic dogs may have a longer childhood than wolves do. Dogs can be trained at any age, but it is very difficult to break bad habits once they have formed. For this reason, a pup should learn 'social' behavior suitable to family pack living as it grows up. It should be taught to defecate in a gutter. And it should be taught not to jump up at people or lick their faces. The owner must act like a firm pack leader as he teaches his dog, and the animal must be rewarded with affection as it learns.

The adult

By the time it is eighteen months to two years old, a dog that has been treated consistently with firmness and affection should be able to take its full place in the human family pack just as the wolf cub does in the hunting team. It should have learned to obey the pack leader, the human owner, and behave in ways that it knows will please the leader in return for his protection and care. In turn the leader should respect the dog's independence and individuality and allow it to live as natural a life as possible: running, sniffing, inspecting other dogs, and playing with its own kind.

Old age

Except for the toy dogs, such as Maltese, Pekinese, miniature poodles and chihuahuas, small breeds tend to live longer than larger dogs. But very few dogs have ever lived more than twenty years; an average lifespan is ten to twelve years. As they grow older dogs will grow more feeble and their sight, hearing and scenting abilities will begin to fade. At this stage of their lives they should be allowed to rest and be protected from younger, more playful dogs. Like humans, dogs suffer from ailments and diseases in their old age. A sick dog is not a happy dog and should be put to sleep.

29

A dog's best friend?

A dog is often called a man's best friend, and rightly so, for what other animal would make such a useful ally? Certainly not the domestic cat, which is solitary by nature and prefers to walk alone. Man long ago gave up his attempts to master it and some early peoples decided to make it an idol of worship instead.

Few civilisations have worshipped dogs or their ancestors the wolves. Yet they have been of far greater value to human beings. In the early days they guarded man's camps and helped him to survive by hunting. In the future, as more is learned about their reactions to travel in outer space, they may journey with us to other planets where their senses may again prove superior to our own and once more contribute to our survival.

While we provide love and protection for all this faithful service, it cannot always be said that we, in turn, are the dog's best friend. In selective breeding, fads and fancies have begun to overtake good sense in many cases. While the long graceful lines of the Shepherd may please show-judges, the selective breeding necessary to achieve these lines sometimes causes a flattening of the hip joints making it hard for the animals to walk. St. Bernard's have been so interbred that some now suffer from nervous diseases. Some other dogs suffer from blindness for the same reason.

As for wolves, once tamed and welcomed into man's camps, they are now ruthlessly persecuted in some countries. They are shot, poisoned and trapped by man in order to stop them from killing livestock. While this protects some sheep and cattle, it also prevents wolves from fulfilling the role that nature intended for them: to act as natural checks on the population of wild grazing animals. Without wolves to kill some of them off, the herds grow bigger and ravage the landscape.

Some countries do have laws to protect the wolf. In these areas scientists will be able to make further studies of wolf behavior. In this way we may learn even more about the reasons why domestic dogs behave as they do.